To Mr. Munoz who helped me find my one true love

Introduction: Why I Had to Write This Book

I have dreamt of being an author. Not to become famous, but to share my passion with the world. When emotions are too much, words are enough.

The sea embodies life. Sometimes you drown and sometimes you swim. Sometimes you get drug under just to come up gasping for air.

I want people to know that they are not alone.

That when nothing makes sense in their life, these words do.

If you have ever experienced

Pain

Love

Heartbreak

Sadness,

Come explore the madness.

Poetry is my rock,
Feelings I cannot explain are
A whole new world.

No judging,
No running,
Just me and my words.

I come to you with words
Full of heart, wisdom, and courage.

Anyone can write,
Most people will not do it
But belief will.

To those who have lost a loved one:

They say time heals all. But what I've found to be true is that time creates space between the initial wound. The wound has left a scar. It does not bleed; it just creates a phantom limb. I tend to find myself falling back into when they were here. It is like I dreamt and forgot the pain of living in a nightmare. These poems are in memory of Janice Elaine Pruitt, and Jerry Allen Wilson. These poems are for the one who's phantom limb still thinks they are there, to create a space in between the living and the dead.

Classified by what we are,
But who are you to judge?

Full of hate,
Full of anger,
Nothing left except sorrow and grief.

Endless skies,
Endless pain,
Nothing remains.

I sit here succumbing to the pain.

The reality sinks in.

I will never see you again on this
Earth, but I am glad you are in the
one place that takes away all the pain.

 I wish it were not so hard to grieve,

But you are worth every tear I have
cried.

You are worth every heart ache, every
bit of loneliness and sadness.

You left far too big of an impact on
the world, and I know you did not
realize it.

I know you are up their rejoicing with
the Lord,

But I also know Jesus will not let you
raise too much hell up there.

You will be loved,

You will be cherished.

But most of all,

 You will be missed.

The burnt edges crinkle.

The ash finds a way in between my fingers.

Since the first time, I have had a hard time.

Seeing her face in elderly women,

Smelling her cigarette smoke triggers a lump in my throat.

Sadness is a friend of mine.

A friend that tells time, of how long she has been gone.

3 years.

3 years of the friend eating out my happiness, bringing back the longing of her.

Her blazing red hair, crystal blue eyes leave a trace.

Someone I cannot replace.

The first time I experienced sadness, I was lonely.

Empty and depressed.

Her eyes still had a twinkling blue spark to me.

Underneath my dress, was a broken porcelain doll.

The ashes sat before me, deep, dark ashes

Signifying her death.

Memories are what I held on to.

Repetition after repetition is what I only had left.

I clinged onto her demanding red hair,

Her smile that gave me hope.

I was awake now, every person wishing us the best.

I sat still like a statue, lost in my pain.

-continued poem-

Rain blanketed the sky, the thud of
teardrops splashing all around.

I was a porcelain doll, lost because my
pieces were shattered.

In every shattered piece you will find
that is where my secrets hide.

Sadness is like falling into a well with no way out.

Drowning in your tears, screaming let me out.

Crying yourself to sleep, always lost in the

Hope of never land.

To remember the pain that aches inside your heart.

To remember the damage that has done

Is another battle they have won.

Sadness, a secret that we all hide.

A secret that could break what is left inside.

Red lines, scratched eyes,

Just grieving for a place to hide.

In her polka dot dress, she fights for a life.

Her strands of hair descend to the pavement.

Her shadow casts a spell, draping over the well.

The well is occupied with fake lies.

The cries of glee, the crawling of fleas all over make you shiver within.

The devil crawls out and taunts you with sin.

I want a hug from all the people I
cannot see

But are in my dreams

The ones that made it seem like life
was going to be easy.

The ones that aren't here to catch me
when I need it most of all.

The ones I'm most alike

But carry the silent cry

Squeeze me until I can't breathe

Or until I fall asleep.

You do everything you've ever
dreamed of

With the biggest supporters that have
the

Highest seat in the house

But all they get to do is watch

And send you signs

There are no words to measure the
pain

That never goes away

The pain comes in waves

Where I can breathe

When I can't leave.

To those who have lost a loved one,
not due to death, but due to them
having left:

Imagine a world where everyone
stayed. It would be a world full of less
heartbreak. I have been resurrected
from each lover, thinking each one
was the last. These poems are for my
first love, my high-school sweetheart,
and the boy I couldn't save from the
start.

The bass drops, his knee pops.

A wrong turn makes my stomach churn.

I have no words.

His cries overflow into my mind.

I am close to the edge.

There are multiple possibilities, but no answers yet.

I cannot help but think of the worst.

I inhale and exhale.

"Are you okay?", they ask.

And for the first time in a long time, I say no.

My plate is full.

I feel numb.

When he hurts, I hurt,

My face turns red and swells up.

The only thing I can do is throw up.

I tell myself I must be strong,

But it seems wrong.

I lay down in a tub full of water.

It does not help.

He came running back to her, but it
was too late.

She picked herself up, she ran to
safety.

He was the epitome of her hurt.

She bled out her heart to him, but he
left her empty,
In the dark,
abandoned.

She was stuck in the moment with
him.

She was drunk on the idea that only
he could fix her.

She broke herself fighting for them
when he walked away from the start.

The angel consumes the empty
bottles, the shattered pieces.

They pierce her skin, but there is no
pain.
It is only numb.

She is adapted to the wound, but it is
stopped bleeding.

The blood flows into the drain,
drowning a girl I once knew.

I lay quietly next to you in bed.

You are sound asleep, but I watch.

I watch you and how you love me without end.

How you love me gracefully.

How you love me continuously.

I squeeze in under your arm and cuddle you.

I melt into your embrace.

The place I call home.

I am never leaving my home.

My protector, my best friend, my soulmate.

I choose you repeatedly each day.

Lie with me until dawn awakes, so I can feel your sweet embrace.

The grinch's heart was two sizes too small,

Mine was too big.

The grinch's heart eventually grew three sizes,

But what if mine shrinks?

Everyone takes my big heart for granted.

And maybe

Just maybe

Somebody would miss it if it shrunk.

Maybe my heart is so big because of all the pain.

Because my heart knows what it is like to hurt.

And I would not wish that on my worst enemy.

I am tired of people taking and taking from me.

-continued poem-

Maybe I have given to many pieces of
my heart away.

How do I get something back that I
never intended to love?

If I could write like you, I'd tell you
how your eyes remind me of the
ocean.

I'd tell you all my broken pieces want
to be fixed by you.

I'd tell you that I have scars and
bruises, but I know you do too.

I'd tell you funny stories until you
laughed so hard you cried.

I'd tell you that I'd play for keeps.

I'd tell you that I think you hung the
moon and I have a feeling that you
think I do too.

If I could write like you, I would do it
every day.

Because you remind me of how much
I wanna stay.

I was lost in the depths of your skin,
the way you held me when walls were
caving in.

I take a deep breath, but there is no
air.

It feels like I am drowning in my own
flaws, the whispers echoing in the
halls.

I wish somebody would help me out.

Not everybody is good at finding a
way out.

I scream my battle cry, but it is just
another goodbye.

Isn't if fun asking questions?

Why did you disappear like a ghost?

Why don't you ever open up?

Why didn't you ever man up?

Tell me.

Because I stay up all night thinking
about us.

Thinking about which one of us took
the bus on the way out.

I only cry in the shower, where I
cannot be heard.
That I am hurt.

The promises that were supposed to
be kept are empty.

Words are lies and actions are proof
of that.

I continuously put my heart on a
platter except

Splat.

It hits floor and bleeds to death.

A heart that is so full of love beats to
the sound of heartache.

It is attracted to it.

How can a person love without a
heart?

I should have known from the start.

If I could write like you, I'd tell you
that I am sorry.

For breaking your heart.

For all the pain.

For the letting go.

I'd tell you that every little thing
reminds me of you.

I'd tell you that I can't be in our small
town without fighting the urge to
drive by.

I'd tell you that my heart aches for
you.

For the you I first met.

I'd tell you that I love you.

I'd tell you that I planned my life with
you and now it hurst to be alone.

I'd tell you that when that day comes,
I'll be ready.

You asked me what I would do if I
was numb from all the pain you
caused me.

My answer is this.

I will be brave enough to feel the pain,

To allow someone to make me feel
again.

All my nights to remember are with you.

The idea of you, the true genuine you has vanished.

People change and I do not know what to say.

They do their worst until the final say.

Nothing is the same.

I cannot fit into the t-shirt anymore.

The girl I know does not live there anymore.

I want to give you everything back, but the story of us is never ending.

I will keep everything you gave me.

The hurt, the love, the memories.

If you come looking for me, I will be lost in the grey-blue sea.

Try not to get lost looking for me.

They always come back when they realize they are trapped

From whatever it was that they were trying to escape from

Once the guard locks the gate, it is too late.

Decisions are made under pressure, and you cracked the code.

Of how easy it was for me to let go

All my nights to remember are with
you.

The idea of you, the true genuine you
has vanished.

People change and I do not know
what to say.

They do their worst until the final say.

Nothing is the same.

There is no meaning, no effort, just a
ripped-up shirt.

It used to be so comfortable to fit in,
but now the seams have been torn.

I cannot fit into the t-shirt anymore,
so I must toss it in the trash, where I
will not ever look back.

I want to give you everything back,
but each little thing has a memory and
I do not want to forget the moments.

I just want to forget you.

There is always a light on

Even if it flickers

It is still there.

The room is always dark

With a burning sensation for more.

The light is sweating because

Of how long it has burned for others

In the darkness

In the darkness you drown or survive.

I burned for you, and you held my
head under water

When all I wanted to do was swim

Peppertree, you can't miss me

When you are the one that chose

To leave me.

Peppertree, together we had a happy return.

But then you exchanged it for no return.

Peppertree,

Where is the leaf that blew off the tree? The leaf that you had turned over

But have now reattached.

Peppertree,

You need your own tree, to grow your own leaves.

And I can't plant the seeds for you.

Peppertree,

There is a return.

But only you can burn the leaves, to create a good seed.

A list of people in line

Who might find that the gift

You gave them is time

The time in the world

To give me what I deserve

The white lines are blank

Wondering how much time is left in
my bank

Was I a target of all your lovers?

A chaotic mess

That whispered your name

Someone you could hang in your hall
of fame

If I was a trophy,

Then you were my trash.

The stories are unraveling

And there is no going back.

I can bag up all the lies and the letters,

All the things that were never meant
to be mine.

Your lovers remember my name

And want to know if you did the same

And the only thing I recognize is your
name

Someone once asked me

Why you hurt so bad

Out of all people

I've had lovers for ages

But what he had was timeless

I thought I would never feel again

Until I met you

You broke the ice

And I finally felt at home

To let the warmth in

But what I didn't see

Was the crack

You fell through

Trying to take me down with you

Her eyes were like the grey-blue sea,

Always running away from me.

Always wanting to come back to you,

But she would never dare to.

Her smile deteriorates.

It is a shattered, hopeless smile trying
to fool everyone around her.

Her hair transforms into different
colors.

Auburn dances around her world,
trying to fix the broken glass.

I loved the love I gave

The one that people always take.

I loved the way you were shiny and
brand new,

Untouched by all the hurt that was
given to you.

I loved the way you were my escape
until you left

And all that stood was red tape

The love I give is something you'll
always miss.

A time machine that will never exist.

I still see you in my dreams

I still reach to touch you when I sleep

At first it was nightmares

And then I realized I wasn't scared

I still have flashbacks of our memories

The good ones come back more

The bad ones try and hide

But they are the reason that I cried

I want to wish away it all

The lies,

The love,

And how you dropped my heart

As if I hadn't brought you out of the dark.

A year ago, I wrote about you

And now I'm writing about a different you

The you that I missed

Who I thought did me so wrong

Couldn't compare to this

A different you reeled me in

And I tried to catch you all at once

I felt for the eyes that hurt

And I wanted to fill them with love so bad

The laugh that comes after a heartbreak is hard to find

Especially once your mind shuts off the idea of being vulnerable again

You wanted me back, but I didn't compare to what you thought you had.

I gave you the benefit of the doubt and you slowly let me down.

Love bombing

When someone makes you drop everything and makes it seem like it's nothing

When someone promises you the world until their guard drops

And they forget they can't stop every lie that's come out of their mouth

The drought hits and everything quits

The bomb imploded on my heart

And what was supposed to be love inside came out to bring the tide to rise

Letting go is like walking on a tightrope

You hang on until you have no choice but to fall

Fall into the truth

Of who you were

And how I denied it

I took your name to the grave

Hoping you'd change

But I realized that's not a reason to stay

It's grounds to walk away

I have held funerals for the men I
loved

Not because they are dead

But that version of them is

Love is not isolating

Love is not demanding

Love is not manipulating

Love does not make you feel crazy

It is supposed to tame you

Love is easy.

Love is kind.

My love will always be mine

And you will die on this shrine.

To the one who has been strong for too long:

I wish someone would've told me that being strong can also be a weakness. Refusing to feel your emotions is not a strength. Life is too beautiful to not feel everything it has to offer.

I look in the mirror.
What do I see?
A pair of eyes staring back at me.

I glance up and
see myself.
What is left,
What is there
What is to become of me.

Scars, and bruises are what is left of
me.
Each scar tells a story.
Each bruise feels pain.
That is what character contains.

How many things have changed?
I find myself alone.
I am trying to find myself.
I feel like a drone.

I used to be carefree,
I used to always be full of glee.
Now I have learned how to stay out
of the way,
How to barely hang on, but just by an
edge.

I will collapse and plummet off the
edge.
The edge of loneliness.
The edge of emptiness.
Please save me from this madness.

She laughs like a god, her mind invisible.

Pick it up.

Start again.

Not every beginning has to end.

One heart,

One brain,

One way to be who you want to be.

Escape it all.

Bring me the morphine, I cannot take the pain.

I am addicted to the way you take it away,

Just like the sky cries when it rains.

So take one last look at me.

Because that is the thing about pain.

It demands to be heard,

it is meant to hurt.

I am on the other side of the moon,

Talking trying to get to you.

Sometimes I feel like a ghost

Living an out of body experience

Due to all my grievances

But the demands are heavy

And there is no break

So I save face

And do what it takes

The word is insensitive to hurt.

Because that is all that lives in it.

The hurt was created in society and hasn't left.

And I am considered weak.

Weak because I have things that I haven't healed from.

And somehow that's my fault.

It is not my job to explain myself.

And the world has no say in what I can and cannot react to.

But we let it anyways.

I hurt in silence and keep secrets,

Because it's easier that way.

Your feelings are valid.

People don't know how you hurt.

Or who or what hurt you.

We are sensitive to what broke us and that is okay.

We are all broken pieces of people and things.

And somehow it is all a puzzle.

Some pieces don't fit right, they have crooked edges.

Some are forced into the designated spot.

Maybe it's okay for someone to figure out how to solve it.

And that is victory in itself,

To make sense to someone else.

I sit and stand,

Waiting for anyone to watch me.

I wave and smile,

While everyone returns the favor.

But do they know?

That I am just a liar

And this world is cruel.

They ask how are you today?

So, I say just fine,

But looks can be deceiving.

I have never understood why people commit suicide.

I have always thought it was selfish.

My mom told me that they are not trying to be, they are just trying to escape the pain.

And one day it clicked.

The pain is invisible until it is not.

Then it becomes unbearable.

The silence becomes too quiet.

The black hole consumes you.

Not all at once, but in slow pieces.

I am a happy person.

I do not want to die; I want to live.

I just want to escape the pain.

I am drowning and all I need is a gasp of air.

A hug.

Someone to talk to.

Not all the time.

Just when I am having a moment and the black hole is trying to consume me.

-continued poem-

Do not label me crazy.

Do not tell me I need help.

Because all I am trying to do is survive
in this living hell.

She tried to pour the cup to the top,

But it was never fulfilled.

Nothing was ever right,

Nothing was ever perfect.

It was simply weird.

The tears fall from the clouds,

An explosion that haunts her dreams.

Her world full of screams.

She sits by herself at the bar, trying to
mend all the scars.

She feels all fuzzy and warm, but she
is lost.

Lost in the adventures, the memories.

Please stop the screaming.

I have hope in the unknown

To bring the light out and wash away
the drones

To drown the darkness

And create madness

A world full of luminescence

Something no one in this world has
witnessed

I have hope that the things I do not
know

will save me from jumping off the
tight rope

I don't know what I feel

Or if I feel at all

It feels like I'm walking on eggshells

On top of a brick wall

The chances of me falling are one to two

Will it hurt less if I try to lose?

I want to win but I don't know how

All I hear are complaints coming from each direction

I wonder if I even have a cheering section

Who roots for me when I don't root for myself?

Who bets on me when others try to push me down?

Who takes my name to the grave when others write my death date?

So many chances to fail

So many chances to learn

So many people in the world

So many voices to be heard

A chance to try something new

A choice that you never knew

A world to open up the doors

A voice that could send a message

Our wreckage gives us purpose

To look beneath the surface

I am afraid to write the feelings I
cannot describe.
To be heartbroken,
To love,
And to hate are all a crime.

I am tired of being my own prisoner,
In my own cell.
It is a living hell.

I countdown the days by tiles.
One,
Two,
Three,
Four,
Five is a year
That you would have been mine.

If I had known you would leave me,
I would have been begging on my
knees for you to stay.

I lay in my cell,
Waiting for you to hear me yell.

I throw myself on the cold floor to
wake up
From this bad dream.
But I wake up with another bruise,
Another scar,
Trying not to tear myself apart.

Waiting and watching for the
breakdown, everyone is on you.

Keep your head up, be tough.

Your flowers are falling unto the
fading memories.

The flowers grow until they give up.

Nothing left to give, no hope, just
another sign of surrender.

The walls cave in, whispering to give
in.

But you my dear, you are special, one
of a kind.

Yet how could I give up when there is
so much life.

Fallout of the trance, society wants
you to dance

Into surrender of the fallout.

To the one who has unspoken monsters:

Everyone has something. Some might keep you up at night. Some might hide under your bed. Some might live in your head. Whatever it may be, keep fighting. When the monsters come out and they continue to be loud, don't back down.

shoot me, I dare you.

The fake, the ugly, everyone will see.

With your hand on the trigger, you
smile

And pull it.

I fall back into the state of unknown.

Angry,

Hurt,

Lost and lonely with a world

Full of people who cannot comfort.

The fence holds me back.

Its barriers confine me and leave me
with
Just enough room to breathe.
My mind is blank.
I cannot even remember my name
anymore.
The fence speaks to me.
He reminds me of every fear, and
every
Flaw I have.
Happiness is not a feeling anymore,
It only exists in the alive human flesh.
I am dead.
My tissue is rotten and black.
The heart is still left with a hint of red.
Red is the hope that remains.
Red is the hope that I will survive.
It is the fire inside of me that will not
back down.
The fence gate fastens itself shut,
leaving me secluded.
I want to breathe again; I want to feel
alive.
But what if the burning of the dead
flesh heals the fence?
What if the burning slowly kills me,
but is worth the pain?
I run until I feel the piercing.
The fence feeds off my blood like an
angry monster.
And I feed off the negativity, as if it is
my future.

I do not need a light to see.
I just need a melody.
I will dance and sing, like there is
nobody watching.

Can I clear my slate?
I never meant to do it.
It was the monster inside me.
The monster that killed everything.

It pierced my skin, so I finally gave in.
I wish I could wake up and
Forget the way you looked at me with
your puppy dog brown eyes.
Pleading for me back, I am so sorry I
got off track.

I am latching on to the chandelier and
holding on for dear life.
I am going to fly like an owl at night,
where no one can see me,
But I am always in sight.

The leaves slowly fall of the tree.

One by one, they jump down.

Trying to get away from the sound.

The monster demolishes the sane.

The breaking windowpane, the crying
of the insane,

Vibrate through the walls of the cell.

The needle pierces the skin,

The needle suppresses the sin.

The monster returns for more.

The monster wants the core.

Void spaces surround the victim.

Spaces that were forgotten,

Spaces that are now rotting.

Being isolated for an extended period,

Leaves you longing for a rewind
button.

The jumpsuit is the only thing that
provides a sense of home.

Finally, comfortable in their own skin.

But the cell guard makes the victim
change their jumpsuit multiple times.

Stripping them of their identity.

Leaving the void spaces,

More time to grow into monsters.

Monsters that provide your demons,

Monsters that leave you dreaming.

The black and white piano keys
Play a melody of the sounds
That feel me with despair.

Gasping for air
The black cord
Wrapping around me
No way out,
No way in.
Lost within.

Wondering the halls,
Exploring my new walls.
I run to the echo,
To find myself.

Two reflections of me,
Fake and real.
As I decide what to choose
The black cord chooses for me
As I fall
Just another teardrop in a waterfall.

I am in an ebony pit, searching for
light.

Searching for luminescence.

I am drowning in the pit of void.
The pit that consumed me,
The pit that concealed my warmth.

There is no fire anymore.
There is no burning flame full of
passion.

There is a spark trying to start a fire,
Trying to start a riot.

Violet helps me remain stable.
Red triggers the anger building up.
And yellow tried to make me keep
The warm love.

You do not know me,

And never will.

The rest are just easy kills.
You think I am the perfect girl.
But do you know who you are talking
to?

I am the devil in disguise,
Someone you should not guide.

I am the owl at night,
Awake in the dark
Cold disguise.

The picture

Who is behind it

The people that have witnessed
milestones in my life

Have walked out

I complete the picture

But there are so many missing puzzle
pieces

The memories that have a hold on me

But I was always responsible for
creating the magic

When the people behind it were just
bystanders

Pull me out of the depths, I feel that I am finally finished.

I got reeled in too fast,

Maybe I am just not a good enough catch.

the knife ricochets off the wall, sending waves across the chamber.

I glance around to find emptiness.

I could do it.

A sharp pain ignites in me, and I collapse on the hard stone floor.

I wake up as a ghost, just the way I was known.

My family stands there, weeping about my death.

My friends gather around cherishing all the good memories.

But you.

You stand in the back, looking away.

Looking away from me because you cut me out.

Cut me off.

I am not a switch.

You cannot keep flicking the light on and off.

-continued poem-

But this time I am off for good.

You stand like a statue.

I am waiting and watching to see what
you do.

He walks out, feelings roaring up
inside.

He knows I am not coming back from
the dead,

He walks out on me like he always
did.

I do not owe you anything.

Not an explanation,

Not a story.

This town whispers who I used to be.

Who I was,

What I did,

And the pieces left of me.

I do not know why I changed.

One day the switch stopped turning
on,

Leaving me with no choice but to
reinvent myself.

If walls could talk, they would tell you
that I had so many friends.

If walls could talk, they would tell you
I loved without end.

They would tell you about the ones
who stayed through it all.

-continued poem-

The ones who laughed and cried and did it all.

But the walls only speak of history.

They do not speak of loneliness.

They do not speak of being lost.

But they echo my reputation, what is expected of me into the halls.

I want to be free from this weight.

The halls are just a walk down memory lane.

The walls gossip about the old me.

But all that matters if that they never really knew me.

People always leave.

The light is green.

Most people want a look behind the scenes.

The light is yellow

Caution because there is no telling where this might go.

The light is red,

Stop this is the end.

I've always been left behind to clean up the evidence of everyone who made this big mess.

To the one who plays
a part in someone's
story:

We cannot all be the
hero. Sometimes we
are the villain. These
are all based off true
emotion devoted to
the ocean of feelings.
If a person or an
emotion didn't make
sense in my story, I
made a scene where
they fit in.

Sound is vibrating off walls.
But no words at all.

For we are afraid to fall.
Be careless, do your thing.

You are unique.
Fall as if you did not care about
anything.
Even if anything could be everything.

Clad in curiosity

You sit watching and waiting,
Standing still.

Time goes by
As people sit there
Like a bear in midst winter.

He sits sleeping,
Waiting for a new season.
People halt and
Never take time to waltz.

Owls are aware,
While everyone sits and stares.
Imps they are, and chimps that sit.

I notice the luminous glow of the sun,
The blessings I have,
The howl at dark
People who make their mark.
Always moving forward,
No time to be a bore
I make all the marks.
I am a bookmark.

"I love this song!" shouted a girl.
Hips swaying in the dark,
With no limit mark.

I wandered off and had gained
someone.
We stood holding hands, not caring
about anyone.

The night was lit with stars,
Perfect from afar.

Staring into each other's eyes,
We realized this was our destiny.
He sealed it with a kiss.

Wind blowing my hair,
Finally, there is air.
The sun shines on me,
I smile.

Peace fills the world,
My thoughts swirl.
I observe my surroundings,
Which are bound to me.

The birds sing a melody,
A melody they can understand.
We are all diverse,
Language, race, and color.

I see beyond myself,
With curiosity I peek.
Nothing weak,
Nothing strong.

Built with memories,
That tag along.
I embrace the new me,
I breathe.

He shouted, "Get out!"
"No" she simply replied.
He slung everything.
Even the flower that sprouted.

"What about us?" she asked
nervously.
"There was never and us. Just you and
me
Trying to be happy," he said.
"Oh," her voice faded.

He entered their room
And retrieved the 22 gauge.
He looked at her in disgust,
He had lost her trust.

Armed with nothing but hatred,
He took aim upon her heart.
Love that would have been
Suddenly fell apart.

The little girl draws with her chalk.

The boy plays with his cars.
And they both collide.

His car runs over her chalk,
She draws the hulk on his car.

Every day for eighteen years.
They repeat it all over again.

Until one day, the boy does not go.
She waits but loses hope.

She runs to his house,
And knocks on the door
To find out it was worth opening the
door.

He had leukemia,
A demon that would slowly kill him.

She held his hand until the end.
When it beeped, she did not know
what to do,
Because he was all she ever knew.

The snow blankets the ground.

The white ghost leaves the crystals,

It leaves a pistol.

The branches shake and crumble.

The branches are like an arrow.

They pierce the skin with a slight touch,

The crisp blood washing up to flood.

There is a light in the tree.

It freezes until there is a she.

She flies with grace; it is almost like a race.

A race to the finish line, a race to end time.

The blood drops off the branch and into the snow.

Let the sweet angel go.

I asked you a question.
You replied, "I have an answer."
Do the flowers bloom?
Does the sun shine?

Do you remember when you were
mine?
Are you always a fake?
You caused me a heartbreak.
"How are you" he asked me,
"I'm fine" I replied.

Fine meaning.
Hurt,
Damaged,
Worthless.
I regret nothing less.

Do you always ignore your exes?
Do you always ignore my texts?
Remember when?

They hold hands and jump in the rain
puddles.
The grey walls cave in, the curtain
falls.
It blocks the light from coming in at
all.
As they splash in the puddle, the
riptide blows.

The water sprays and explodes.

The rain beats down, all I want you to
do is come around.

Let us go back to when we were kids,
back to everything we all miss.

She had a glimmer in her eye that no
one could explain.
She said, "I'm tired, take me home."
But they always said make more room.

Got lost in the muse,
Just coloring outside the lines.

Take me aside,
Throw me to the lions.
I am just an animal waiting for more.

The lions sit and pounce, waiting for
the moment
One,
Two,
Three,
She is gone.

Put away for good.
Knowing they could have had it all.

We paid it in our blood,
Because what is more vulnerable than
you?

She put on her wings

And he taught her how to fly.

He gave her lessons,

Because she could not deny.

She thought the love would last,

To find out everything changes.

And it was never the same.

The fox waits for his prey,
Nothing comes,
He gets astray.

His devilish glare
Only attracts me,
The innocent hare.

He sits staring at me,
Until I strut over.
I bring myself,
He sits there on his shelf.

I step back,
And realize there are other tracks.
He stares at me with his devilish grin
As I fall in.

I was trapped
With only a map.

Every flower blooms,

Every bride has a groom.
Everything connects, so complex.

A flower dies,
The groom fades away,
The end hiding in the shades.

A cycle begins again
Never having an end.
The end jumps out and surprises you.

Takes away,
Starts a new day.
Every beginning has an end,
Every end has a beginning.

I took a walk across the land,

I knew it like the back of my hand.

The trees whisper our secrets,

And the birds sing our song.

Tell me your regrets.

Tell me where we belong.

I am tired of being unknown,

Just tell me where to go.

Take me away,

Where only you know my fate.

Because who knew we all fade away?

Each leaf slowly drops after one
another.

It is like we are playing dominoes

The friends insult each other.

The piano escalates.

Lies are built on a solid foundation.

The piano is playing so hard, it is
almost at it is breaking point.

They drag each other down.

The piano breaks.

No one is there to pick up the pieces.

Years pass.

The dominoes glare at me.

They tell me that I was not there when
they needed help.

But they were never there when I fell.

I grasped onto anything to pick myself
up.

While I am on my feet, standing on a
built foundation, all of you are still
pushing each other down.

Down into the depths, where no one
can pull you out

-continued poem-

Because there is a hole dug deep
down.

You must be big and bold, so that we
can hear you out in the cold.

Just want to throw my hair back

Remember those good old tracks
Not a care in the world,
Just me.

I hear my name and run to the sound.
It was only the echo of my voice.
I scream at the sky just to listen.
My voice is a cloud.

It rains,
Its soft,
It mumbles,
Just like a cloud when it stumbles.

Blood pumping,
I jump.

Into an empty space that fills my
thoughts.

The black chalk board wall is covered
in signatures.

The chalk smears into the gradually
faint light.

The colors of the rainbow dance on
the wall.

ROYGBIV falls.

The colors detach.

There are no good spirits.

There is no joy.

It is just a group of friends that do not
care.

Their decisions reflect themselves, so
they leave out yellow.

There is no rainbow anymore.

Just a splat of yellow on the floor.

Everyone stomping on the décor.

Her red hair ignites a fire.

A fire that is too monstrous for the flames to stop.

It never stops.

Her flames make her seem dangerous

"Don't mess with me", they scream

But no one ever listens.

The fire builds up until it is an inferno.

Everything catches on fire.

She screams "Let's go!"

She leaves without them and there is a big mess for them to clean up.

Her flames are her signature

Her signature of life.

Her signature of death.

Try to catch your breath.

We live in shades of blue

From morning dew to nightfall

The sky dictates it all.

From blue jeans to faded screams

From light wash to dark wash

From ripped to whole.

Something resonates with my soul.

From normal cycle to heavy

Put me in the dryer no matter the
time.

From an hour to twenty minutes, the
fire will be dried out.

Repeat the cycle.

Toss me up and throw me out.

I want to be as brand new as when
you put me in the cycle.

The cycle of being dirty, and the need
to be cleaned.

Because once you are washed and
dried for the first time, you will never
be new again.

To those who love without end:

Love is like screaming, crying, and throwing up all at the same time. Love is a series of sharing your wounds and hoping that somebody will heal them. But sometimes we come out of love with a deeper cut than before. To love is to feel, and I hope you never go numb.

A four-letter word with different
meanings.
Always in sync no matter what.

Searching for something unknown,
I found you, together we are known.
We stick like glue, never tearing apart.

Faithfully our relationship
Progresses eternally.
I was broken
Suddenly together
We mended it back together.

Love is forgiving when nothing is left
to give.
Love is anything one shares with
something.

Loving the precious moments you
share,
For we are unable to tear.
Different people
Who knew we complete each other?

Love is something special.
Love is something clean.
Love is the spaces in between.
Everlasting be my prince, for I have
Known you ever since.

A positive and negative,
We both bring out in each other.
Ups and downs, love is profound.

-continued poem-

Committed you must be, not running
away with glee.
Love is pure, forever it will endure.

Love is friendship,
Love is lean,
Love is leaning on someone when you
are in need.

Your hair,
Your eyes.
Your perfect in every disguise.

Forever one,
Forever two,
Forever the one who loves you.

Accept their flaws, no one is perfect.
Love their flaws every second of the
day,
Who cares what people say?

You must trust him.
Trust is what a relationship is

-continued poem-

Communicate you must, always trust.

Joy when I open your good morning
texts,
Wondering what will happen next.
Your hand fits perfectly in mine, they
combine every time.

Looking into your eyes,
Staring deep down into what is mine.

Flirting with each other is what we do
best,
Who would detest?

A four-letter word,
Brings our worlds together.
Love is this,
Love is that,
Our worlds collapse.

We are one,
We are whole,
Now the future unfolds.

Not enough words,
Not enough spaces,
To share how much, we have
engaged.

Dear someone,
Are you out there?
Do you remember my hopes and
fears?
You could always dry my tears.
Now they are overflowing, and I
cannot control it.

Because you still have the key.
The key to my heart, the key to a new
start.

I was wrong, and now I am wondering
the streets all alone.
Wondering the streets, I used to
know.

I almost pick up the phone, to let you
know I wish it was the same.
Maybe you are on the end of the line,
just waiting for time.

I took the time to sit down and accept
the fact I am alone.

I am sorry to say, I cannot even
remember your name.
I poured the kerosene all around.
I was hoping I would never find you.

How did we get here?
I can figure it out on my own.

Here is a note,
Here is the mystery,
And here is the code.

So, baby crack me.
It might be hard,
but mysteries are classic.

You started a fire,
It built until I could not be wilted
anymore.
A flower is bright
A flower is nice.

I once was a bee,
You came and killed my buzz.
The fire expanded,
You left me stranded.

Sticks and stones broke my bones,
But your words always hurt me.
A friend saved me.
He built me strong,
Always prepared when something
went wrong.

He saved a place for me.
His heart.
Side my side,
Walking with the light.

You are my partner,
You stayed during the fire.

I do not understand.
How do you move on?
I have heard that you have got a secret
Way to do it.

You go to the next girl,
Like she is a prize.
You tell her she is the best,
Just like you have told the rest of us.

I am just another memory.
Another reason for you to kill me.

Take your dagger out and
Slice me to pieces.
It will be easier for us to move on.
You are already out the door and
I am long gone.

I am getting on the train to Frisco,
You do not even care if I go.
Watch me as I get up and leave.
I blow you a kiss,
Which is all you will ever receive.
I'm just another secret and you are a
mystery.

Tears crash down, I stand my ground.

They say it is just a scratch, but will I
ever get it back?

I play my guitar til my fingers bleed
The pain is my remedy.

How can something you love hurt so
much?

The tears form into a puddle, then a
sea.

The depths getting deeper and deeper
until
I can no longer see.
You're going to have to swim out and
rescue me.
Or leave me to drown, for the sharks
to eat my cold
Hard flesh.

Her tears drip from her delicate face.

They land on her pillow,

The land of 1000 sorrows.

Her pillowcase is sopping wet from all
the tears.

Nothing can soak up her broken
heart.

It will never be mended.

Her heart breaks into a million pieces
just trying to figure everything out.

Trying to figure out which one gave
up on this hopeless love.

The love that haunts her dreams at
night,

The love that makes everything
alright.

Standing on the corner, just a little
late.

Where were you?

I think you have lost your mind, but
we all need time.

Clock goes tick,
Everything clicks.

Open your ears, can you hear me?
I scream your name; it always sounds
the same.

Sending you notes from the back of
the class,
It seems like there is a wall of glass.

I write goodbye, my feelings knotted
up inside.

I stop and wait; this love is strange.

I drop the pencil, and erase.

Because I always come back to you.

All I do is give out second chances
and maybe

I am wrong for that.

The missed calls, unanswered
messages make me think

What if?

Forgiving is not easy, but I will always
remember what you did.

I thought I was different to you, but
you treated me like the others.

Like I am supposed to blend in.

I love you is three words.

Three words that can mean nothing.

Three words that can mean the world.

I have only said I love you to one
person

And that is you.

The difference is I meant it,

But did you?

New things and

Old things are the same.

New as the winter snow,
Old as dead grass.
Pick the one that stayed
With you longest
And never left your grasp.

But everyone deserves one last
chance.
Out with the old, in the new.
As I do not agree.

Out with the new, in with the old.
Whoever came and stayed should

grow old with you.

I am just a big storm, lightning and
thunder combined.

Eventually love dies.

It fades away into the black hole.

You cannot retrieve it back.

Sometimes three lucky chances are not
enough.

You must give them a whole lifetime.

And I do not know if I can keep
trying.

Trying to understand when they
repeat the same mistakes over again.

Trying not to feel resented when they
do not pay attention to you anymore.

I want the best for you, but
sometimes I am not always the best
option.

Or maybe I just was not good enough
to begin with.

The end turns into a symphonic
melody.

The piano keys crescendo, building up
to the climax.

It slows descends, leading to the
melody.

The part that always gets me.

The broken record dies faithfully.

The journals stayed sealed in a secure
case.

The pages are full of ink.

The ink that started it all.

There are dried tears in the journal.

You tell him all your stupid boy
stories.

He laughs with the brightest smile on
his face.

The brown eyes sparkle, his eyes light
up with a burning flame.

His faults are perfection, everything
about him is right.

-continued poem-

I was afraid to love and start over.

To open and let him mend my broken heart.

The waves come to shore, and I jump in freely.

I jump far into the crazy tide.

I am not here to occupy your time.

I am not here to be your play toy.

I am here to be something.

Hear me out,

Shut me out.

Give me a reason to stay.

I am not used to being stomped in the ground.

I would ask for a hug, but I might die.

You took what was inside.

Just return it, and I will be alright.

I used to love him, but I had to kill him.

So when I close my eyes,

Look deep down in the ground to find me.

Buried and breathing.

Just give me a reason.

I never promised I would let go.

I promised I would be there for you,
even when you did not know.

I turned the hourglass over.

60 seconds to reveal our ghosts.

60 seconds to shatter the ones that
you love the most.

Everything I touch turns into dust.

It is what happens when there is no
one you can trust.

She blows out the candles, leaving the
room empty.

The crime scene is left without any
evidence.

Except for one candle she forgot to
blow out.

She tries to go to sleep, but now she is
diagnosed with insomnia.

A wicked, sinful place she would
never understand.

The shadows around her eyes come from sleepless nights.

The insomnia has possessed her soul.

Her eyes tell a story.

The story of why she never sleeps.

The story of the catastrophes she has been through.

They never ask, but always stare.

Her hair has dark streaks.

It is the story of the shrieking, torn heart.

It has been lit up and it has been blown out.

Blown out of creation, leaving the ashes for the next hidden soul.

Her skin is soft like a delicate porcelain doll.

Everyone wants to touch it, but they are too scared.

Her skin aches of love.

Something that has been gone.

-continued poem-

Something that everyone longs.

Her lips tell the secrets.

Her lips tell the story.

The story no one wants to hear.

It is a curse.

A curse luring them in,

A curse that might destroy everything
within.

The best part is she never says a word.

The people know she has a sword, a
sword of gold.

The burdens form a hole deep down
in her soul.

Are we weak for feeling?

or

Are we brave for feeling?

Are we weak for letting go?

or

Are we brave for moving on?

Are we weak because we are
struggling?

or

Are we brave because we ask for help?

Am I weak because you made me this
way?

or

Is it because my broken pieces never
stay?

Am I brave for riding the wave?

Or walking away?

Do I hide my deck

Until you put all of your cards

On the table

Do I hide my king

Until you are all in

Do I fall into sin

Do I fall into the way

That you play your ace

Are you bluffing until the cards

Are stacked against me

Are you waiting until I can longer win

Deal me in

Love yourself.

Because if you do not do it,

No one else will.

Love yourself because life is too short
not to.

Learn to love the things you hate
about yourself.

Love the way that you love.

Hard,

Fast,

And all at once.

Do not change the way you love
because of how you have been
wronged in the past.

Let it go and love the next person
even harder.

-continued poem-

The world needs more of your love.

So make sure you save enough love
for yourself,

Before you give it all away.

What if rejection is the exception that we are whole without the approval of others?

What if we accepted ourselves before trying to give someone a say if they choose to stay?

What if we gave ourselves grace when we aren't accepted or loved?

What if a setback is all that's ever stood in the way of true love?

Age is just a number

That reflects our character

An old soul sticks to tradition

While the younger generations want a rendition.

I don't want a show for the whole world to see,

Just something special for you and me.

I want someone to love

The loud and the quiet.

And to make everything alright.

Not to impress people

Not to please people

To keep the tradition going

Of how loves stays alive til the end of time

Acknowledgment:

Thank you to anyone who has ever read my poetry. Thank you to Mr. Munoz for helping me discover an outlet for my feelings. Thank you to my family for always supporting me.Thank you to Brian Lyke for being the first one to listen about the idea of writing and designing my own book and for encouraging me along the way. Thank you to everyone who listened and gave feedback during this whole process. I am so thankful to have a God given talent to share with you all.